The **Pebble** First Guide to

Songbirds

by Katy R. Kudela

Consulting Editor: Gail Saunders-Smith, PhD

Consultant: Laura Erickson, Science Editor
Cornell Laboratory of Ornithology
Ithaca, New York

Capstone
press®

Mankato, Minnesota

Pebble Books are published by Capstone Press,
151 Good Counsel Drive, P.O. Box 669, Mankato, Minnesota 56002.
www.capstonepress.com

1 2 3 4 5 6 14 13 12 11 10 09

Library of Congress Cataloging-in-Publication Data
Kudela, Katy R.
    The pebble first guide to songbirds / by Katy R. Kudela.
    p. cm. — (Pebble books. Pebble first guides)
    Includes bibliographical references and index.
    Summary: "A basic field guide format introduces 13 songbirds. Includes color
photographs and range maps"   Provided by publisher.
    ISBN-13: 978-1-4296-2244-8 (hardcover)   ISBN-10: 1-4296-2244-X (hardcover)
    ISBN-13: 978-1-4296-3442-7 (paperback)   ISBN-10: 1-4296-3442-1 (paperback)
    1. Songbirds — Juvenile literature. I. Title. II. Series.
QL696.P2K83 2009
598.8 — dc22   2008028237

About Songbirds

A songbird is a bird with special feet for perching on branches. Songbirds also have a special voice box to communicate with calls and songs. For most kinds of songbirds, only the males sing. Songs warn other males to stay away. Songs also help male songbirds find a mate.

Note to Parents and Teachers

The Pebble First Guides set supports science standards related to life science. In a reference format, this book describes and illustrates 13 songbirds. This book introduces early readers to subject-specific vocabulary words, which are defined in the Glossary section. Early readers may need assistance to read some words and to use the Table of Contents, Glossary, Read More, Internet Sites, and Index sections of the book.

Table of Contents

Height:	16 to 21 inches (41 to 53 centimeters)
Wingspan:	33 to 39 inches (84 to 99 centimeters)
Eats:	insects, seeds, grains, fruit, garbage
Lives:	open areas with a few trees
Facts:	• stores food in hiding places
	• mates for life

American Crow Range

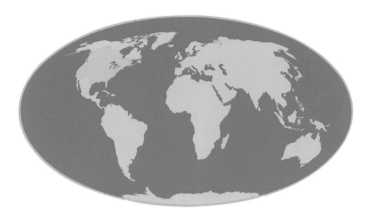

☐ North America

young crows

American Goldfinch

male

female

Height:	4 to 5 inches (10 to 13 centimeters)
Wingspan:	7 to 9 inches (18 to 23 centimeters)
Eats:	seeds
Lives:	weedy fields, orchards, gardens
Facts:	• builds nest with thistle seeds • sometimes called the wild canary

American Goldfinch Range

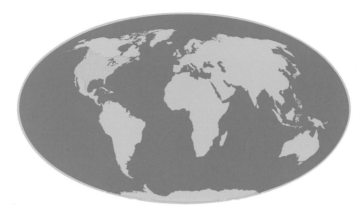

☐ North America

young

American Robin

eggs

Height:	8 to 11 inches (20 to 28 centimeters)
Wingspan:	12 to 16 inches (30 to 41 centimeters)
Eats:	earthworms, insects, fruit
Lives:	forests, woodlands, gardens
Facts:	• young robins have spotted breasts • easily sees earthworms in their holes

American Robin Range

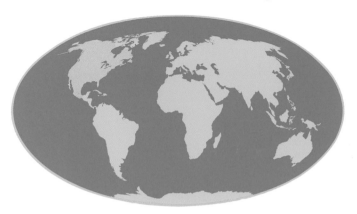

☐ North America

adult with chicks

Height:	7 to 8 inches (18 to 20 centimeters)
Wingspan:	9 to 12 inches (23 to 30 centimeters)
Eats:	caterpillars, fruit, insects, nectar
Lives:	open areas with a few tall trees
Facts:	• nest hangs from outer tree branches • also called the golden robin

Baltimore Oriole Range

☐ North America, Central America, South America

male

nest

female

11

Black-capped Chickadee

Height:	5 to 6 inches (13 to 15 centimeters)
Wingspan:	6 to 8 inches (15 to 20 centimeters)
Eats:	insects, seeds, berries
Lives:	forests, open areas with large trees
Facts:	• remembers thousands of places where it hides food
	• can survive freezing cold winters

Black-capped Chickadee Range

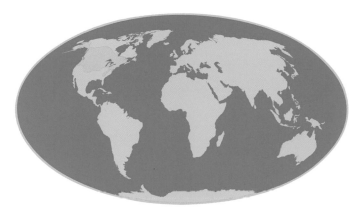

☐ North America

chicks

Blue Jay

Height:	10 to 12 inches (25 to 30 centimeters)
Wingspan:	13 to 17 inches (33 to 43 centimeters)
Eats:	insects, nuts, fruit, seeds
Lives:	oak trees
Facts:	• screeches like a hawk
	• mates for life

Blue Jay Range

☐ North America

adult with young

15

Eastern Bluebird

female

male

Height:	6 to 8 inches (15 to 20 centimeters)
Wingspan:	10 to 13 inches (25 to 33 centimeters)
Eats:	insects, small fruit
Lives:	orchards, parks, pastures
Facts:	• nests in holes in trees • some nest in birdhouses

Eastern Bluebird Range

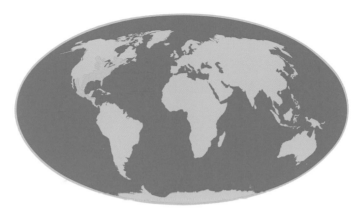

☐ North America, Central America

eggs

adult with young

House Finch

female

male

Height:	5 to 6 inches (13 to 15 centimeters)
Wingspan:	8 to 10 inches (20 to 25 centimeters)
Eats:	buds, seeds, fruit
Lives:	spruce trees, oak trees, grasslands
Facts:	• colors in food make males' feathers yellow or red
	• build nests in hanging plant baskets

18

House Finch Range

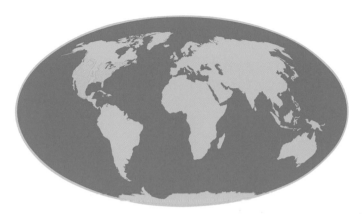

☐ North America

adults with chicks

19

Indigo Bunting

male

Height:	5 to 5.5 inches (13 to 14 centimeters)
Wingspan:	7 to 9 inches (18 to 23 centimeters)
Eats:	insects, spiders, seeds, buds, berries
Lives:	hedgerows, fruit trees, weedy fields
Facts:	• adult males look brown in fall and winter
	• migrates at night and follows the stars

20

Indigo Bunting Range

☐ North America, Central America, South America

female with chicks

Northern Cardinal

female

male

Height:	8 to 9 inches (20 to 23 centimeters)
Wingspan:	10 to 12 inches (25 to 30 centimeters)
Eats:	seeds, fruit, buds, insects
Lives:	shrubs, small trees
Facts:	• both males and females sing
	• state bird of seven U.S. states

Northern Cardinal Range

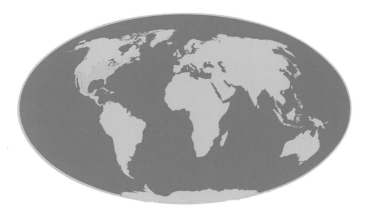

☐ North America, Central America

female with chicks

Northern Mockingbird

Height:	8 to 10 inches (20 to 25 centimeters)
Wingspan:	12 to 14 inches (30 to 36 centimeters)
Eats:	fruit, insects
Lives:	thickets, desert brush, shrubs
Facts:	• males copy new songs and sounds
	• females do not sing much

Northern Mockingbird Range

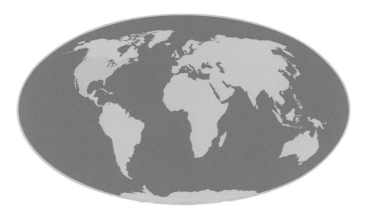

☐ North America, Caribbean islands

adult with chicks

Red-winged Blackbird

male

Height:	7 to 9 inches (18 to 23 centimeters)
Wingspan:	12 to 16 inches (30 to 41 centimeters)
Eats:	insects, seeds, grains
Lives:	marshes, meadows, alfalfa fields
Facts:	• named for red patches on adult male
	• often builds nest near water

26

Red-winged Blackbird Range

☐ North America, Central America

female with chicks

White-breasted Nuthatch

Height:	5 to 6 inches (13 to 15 centimeters)
Wingspan:	8 to 11 inches (20 to 28 centimeters)
Eats:	insects, nuts, seeds
Lives:	maple trees, birch trees, oak trees
Facts:	• climbs down tree trunks headfirst
	• flies with chickadee flocks in winter

White-breasted Nuthatch Range

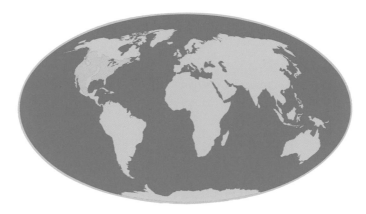

☐ North America

nest hole

Glossary

alfalfa — a type of grass

bud — a small shoot on a plant that grows into a leaf or a flower

flock — a group of the same kind of animal; members of flocks live, travel, and eat together.

hedgerow — a narrow strip of trees and shrubs that often divides fields

marsh — an area of wet, low land

migrate — to move from one place to another

nectar — a sweet liquid that some insects or birds collect from flowers and eat as food

orchard — a field or farm where fruit trees are grown

thicket — a thick growth of plants, bushes, or small trees

thistle — a wild plant

wingspan — the distance between the tips of a pair of wings when fully open

Read More

Gallo, Frank. *Bird Calls*. Hear and There Book. Norwalk, Conn.: Innovative KIDS, 2001.

Tagliaferro, Linda. *Birds and Their Nests*. Animal Homes. Mankato, Minn.: Capstone Press, 2004.

Internet Sites

FactHound offers a safe, fun way to find educator-approved Internet sites related to this book.

Here's what you do:

1. Visit *www.facthound.com*

2. Choose your grade level.

3. Begin your search.

This book's ID number is 9781429622448.

FactHound will fetch the best sites for you!

Index

Grade: 1
Early-Intervention Level: 22

Editorial Credits
Alison Thiele, set designer; Biner Design, book designer; Jo Miller, photo researcher

Photo Credits
Alamy/David Watts, 29; Rick & Nora Bowers, 17 (right); Rolf Nussbaumer, 11 (left);
   Stock Connection Distribution/Peter Bisset, 21
Bruce Coleman Inc./Bob & Clara Calhoun, 19; Jen & Des Bartlett, 5; Joe McDonald,
   11 (right)
fotolia/Bruce MacQueen, 8 (left)
Getty Images Inc./Minden Pictures/Tom Vezo, 23
iStockphoto/Alain Turgeon, 13 (right); Bill Raboin, 10; Bruce MacQueen, cover
   (blue jay), 12; David Parsons, 26; Frank Leung, 7; Kelly Watson, 13 (left)
Jupiterimages Corporation, cover (eastern bluebird), 9, 27
Shutterstock/Al Mueller, 6 (left); Bob Blanchard, cover (northern cardinal), 14;
   Bruce MacQueen, 28; Bryan Eastham, 20; Glen Gaffney, 6 (right); Jemini Joseph,
   18 (left); Michael J Thompson, 24; Michael Woodruff, 4; RLHambley, 22 (right);
   Steve Byland, 18 (right); teekaygee, cover (goldfinch); Theresa Martinez, 8 (right);
   Tony Campbell, 22 (left); viZualStudio, 17 (left)
Visuals Unlimited/Charles Melton, 25; Gay Bumgarner, 16; John Gerlach, 15

The author dedicates this book to her niece. A world of wonder awaits you, Eleanor!